Follow that Food

Bite Me

by

Chef John St Aubin

Book title by **Ana Quadros.** *Thanks for that Ana.*

Cover Art by **David Brynaert.**

Thanks for that Dave and for the delicious scotch you served me during the process.

Edited by **Cindy Bristow**

Thank you for all your late nights Cyn, getting my grammar right and all the punctuation I missed.

Copyright © 2015 John St Aubin

All rights reserved.

ISBN:1494306557
ISBN-13:9781494306557

Follow that Food

Retired chef: John St Aubin

I dedicate this to all the fans of my cooking throughout the years.

I have changed the names to protect the innocent and also to cover my ass.
Any mistakes I may have made are blamed on the person who found them in my book.
If I am quoting a person or plagiarizing something it's in italics.

CONTENTS

	Introduction	v
1	Spice Mixes	Pg # 3
2	Breakfast/Brunch	Pg# 8
3	Appetizers	Pg # 13
4	Salads and Dressings	Pg# 22
5	Breads	Pg # 31
6	Soups	Pg # 41
7	Sauces	Pg # 49
8	Side dishes	Pg # 61
9	Main Meals	Pg # 68
10	Sausages	Pg# 105
11	Desserts	Pg# 112
12	Drinks	Pg# 129

INTRODUCTION

First of all there are no pictures…. did your granny have pictures on her index cards written in her chicken scratch? So Bite Me!!!! Heh, heh, heh!!!

Now here are the guidelines:

1 Your finger is your best tasting tool. (It was good enough for Auntie Marge).
2 Buy a kitchen scale $10 (I use weights, it's easy and you can tare the scale for each ingredient).
3 I use tablespoons and teaspoons from the cutlery drawer. Plenty of them and you can wash them later.
4 Preparation time (who cares) you live for this anyway; a day in the kitchen is better than a lot of other sh*t

No colored pictures, unless I make a fortune and re-publish.

This is not like other cookbooks; I have tried to keep the blah, blah, blah out of the recipe. In other words they are written the way you prepare, for people who cook.

The page size is US letter so you can print them and put them in a binder. Just print the ones you like and for the ones you don't like, crunch them up into a little ball and pitch them. Don't forget to curse me out and email me with the reason!

I try to keep it on one page if possible.

I have written each recipe the way you would prepare it, so you might see onions or butter appear a few times. Which brings me to why; don't you just love it when they list the items at the top and use different bits of it in several places of the directions or leave out one ingredient completely (so now what do I do with $25 worth of truffles?). How about this one? When you go to make the recipe it just goes; combine the frozen duck beaks, onions, garlic and watermelon seeds, then you have to go back to the list of ingredients to see how much of each you need and you end up missing an ingredient or putting the wrong amount in. *Thanks for that one, Darcy.* If you want a cute little list of things to shop for, "suck it" *Thanks for that one, Penny.* Ok, if you must, just look down the third column and you can see the list of all the ingredients.

In the instructions, if words like: mix, fold, sauté, whisk or deglaze and reduce are unknown to you, just ask somebody else that cooks more than you do or look it up on the web.

I am going to assume you have the basic skills, ingredients and spices hanging around in the cupboards.

I have not bothered with cooking times unless it's important, cook until done, you know when something is done right?

As a retired chef owner of a restaurant, I liked to partition my recipes so you didn't have to do the whole recipe every time. I have the spice blends on hand and some sauces made already. You too can do this on a personal scale, for instance the spice mix for Mexican salsa (Picco de Gallo) can be used for lots of other stuff too. Be experimental, the Mamou sauce is the beginnings of any great cream sauce like Alfredo. Most of the food here can be frozen as well. I use Ziplock bags to portion for single meals and sometimes I can sauces, you know like in jars with lids hahaha.

Tools: I am fortunate enough to have a Kitchen Aid mixer but the rest is basic stuff.

Oven temp is always 350 degrees unless otherwise indicated.

One last thing, my humor, spelling and grammar don't count OK?

YOU MAY HAVE NOTICED THERE IS NO THEME TO MY BOOK AND THE ORDER OF THINGS LOOKS WACKY.

There are lots of different types of foods here.

That's because I have only put in the recipes that I like best so far.

One person actually asked me why I didn't have roast chicken in my book! I just about choked on my cervesa, so I replied to him (Ravi), "Don't worry, you probably shouldn't buy my book."

Any questions, comments, just to say hello, or if you have a killer recipe you want to share:
Email me at
johnst.aubin60@gmail.com

Or on my face book page:
Follow that Food

Follow that Food

Copywrite

Spice Mixes

These are handy if you can't get out to buy them or find them in the stores.
Ok I know you didn't read the intro but if you need to shop for the ingredients, just look down the third column on every page and they will magically appear.

Mild Salsa Spice Mix

½	cup	Cumin
½	cup	Chili powder
¼	cup	Garlic powder
¼	cup	Salt
1 ½	tsp.	Cayenne pepper
1 ½	tsp.	Mustard powder

Gringo Spice Mix

"This makes any food instantly Mexican."

4	TBS	Chili powder
1	TBS	Cocoa
1	TBS	Onion flakes
1	TBS	Cumin
1/2	tsp.	Paprika
1/2	tsp.	Salt
1/2	tsp.	Sugar
1/4	tsp.	Garlic powder
1/4	tsp.	Cayenne pepper

Copyright

Blackened Spice Mix

This should only be used for blackening period.

½	cup	Paprika (and this is the reason---- Bite me)
1	TBS	Onion powder
1	TBS	Garlic powder
1	tsp.	Cayenne pepper
1	tsp.	Black pepper
1	tsp.	Thyme
1	tsp.	Oregano
½	tsp.	Salt

Caribbean Spice Rub

1	TBS	Kosher salt
2	tsp.	Curry powder
2	tsp.	Coriander
2	tsp.	Allspice
1	tsp.	Black pepper
½	tsp.	Nutmeg
½	tsp.	Cumin

Chicken Shake Spice

Deep South style!

¼	cup	Paprika (smoked if possible)
1	TBS	Cumin
1	TBS	Black pepper
3	TBS	Cayenne pepper
¼	tsp.	Cloves ground
½	tsp.	Cinnamon
1	tsp.	Ginger
1	tsp.	Garlic powder
2	tsp.	Celery salt
2	tsp.	Kosher salt

Copyright

Garam Masala

1	TBS	Cumin
1 ½	tsp.	Coriander
1 ½	tsp.	Cardamom
1 ½	tsp.	Black pepper
1	tsp.	Cinnamon
½	tsp.	Cloves
½	tsp.	Nutmeg

Garam Tandoori

1	tsp.	Ginger
1	tsp.	Cumin
1	tsp.	Coriander
1	tsp.	Paprika
1	tsp.	Turmeric
1	tsp.	Salt
1	tsp.	Cayenne pepper

Jamaican Jerk Spice Rub

Ya mon!

1	TBS	Sugar
1	TBS	Minced onion flakes dried
1	TBS	Salt
1	tsp.	Cayenne pepper
1	tsp.	Cinnamon
1	tsp.	Nutmeg
1	tsp.	Allspice
2	tsp.	Thyme

Mamou Spice Mix

I have never tried it on anything but chicken let me know if you experiment?

1 ½	tsp.	Paprika
1	tsp.	Sage
1	tsp.	White pepper
1	tsp.	Onion powder
1	tsp.	Garlic powder
1	tsp.	Cayenne pepper
1	tsp.	Basil
½	tsp.	Black pepper
½	tsp.	Thyme
½	tsp.	Salt

Cajun Curry Spice Mix

1	cup	Flour
½	cup	Curry powder
2	TBS	Cayenne pepper
1	TBS	Cumin
1	TBS	Basil
1	TBS	Salt
1	tsp.	Coriander powder

Breakfasts and Brunch

Huevos Mexicana

Cindy's favorite.

In a saucepan:
Sauté:

1	TBS	Olive oil
1	TBS	Butter or bacon fat
½	cup	Pico de Gallo salsa

Whisk and add:

4		Eggs
1	splash	Milk

Scramble until cooked

Serve with: Flour tortillas warmed up
Jalapeño sauce
Refried beans

Notes: It's ok to write your notes in this book, that's why I left space at the bottom.

Potato and Egg Omelet

Sauté in olive oil:
Stuff you like; spinach, mushrooms, tomatoes, ham, etc. about a cup finished.

Whisk
4		Eggs
¾	cup	Mashed potatoes (leftovers)
Splash of		milk

Pour the whisked egg mix into the sautéed veggies and stir to make it even.
Sprinkle shredded cheese on top.
Garnish with sliced tomato or cherry tomatoes.

Cook on low until starting to firm up around edges

Put in oven until firm and puffed up

Remove from oven when cooked and let rest for 5 min

Ta da !!

Spinach Frittata

Sauté
1	TBS	Butter
1	tsp.	Olive oil
½	cup	Potatoes, sliced or diced

When spuds are almost cooked add and continue to sauté:
1		Green onion sliced
1	cup	Spinach
		Salt and pepper to taste

I usually toss in a splash or two of Worchester sauce, it perks up the spinach flavor. Optional is to also add stuff from your fridge, no rules here.

Whisk:
4		Eggs
3	TBS	Milk

Add:
1/3	cup	Cheddar cheese (or your favorite) shredded

Cook in a non-stick pan on low until it starts firming up then put in the oven until firm, fluffy and cooked.

3-Cheese and Spinach Pie

Make Pastry Recipe: Pg. 117
Roll out to fit pie plate
Half bake crust about 10 min (there are many tricks to this, using dry beans is one)

FILLING
Sauté:

2/3	bag	Spinach (about 4 cups) with a little dash of Worchester sauce

Add and sauté:

1		Green onion chopped
3	TBS	Mushrooms, diced wild ones if you can
1	TBS	Black pepper
2	TBS	Parmesan cheese grated
3	TBS	Feta cheese (heaping) crumbled
½	cup	Cheddar cheese grated

Mix separately:

3		Eggs beaten
1	TBS	Cream
1	TBS	Flour

Mix all this together and place in the piecrust.
Bake for about 30 min or until center is firm.

Thinks you eat before you eat
Appetizers

"Did that come out right?"

Blackened Shrimp

This spice and technique can be used for all blackened foods
Fish, steak or chicken.

Dig out of your cupboard or make:
Blackened spice mix: Pg. 5

Precook thawed shrimp shell on zipper backs in a crawfish boil – 30/40 count.
The ones from Thailand are great.

Crawfish boil:
1		Onion small chopped up
1		Lemon squeezed
1	TBS	Cayenne pepper

Bring water to boil
Add			Shrimps

When water re-boils and the shrimp turn pink, drain, then shock in cold water to stop cooking, peel shells off shrimp, you can leave the tails on it looks nice.

You need to have a good exhaust hood for your range, or cook outside on a BBQ.
Preheat cast iron pan to very hot and have some melted butter available.

Sprinkle the blackened spice mix lightly on the shrimp.
Cook on dry heat and turn over in about 2 min each side. When done brush with melted butter and serve immediately.

For other meats cook each side until done and slobber it with melted butter then serve immediately.
The finished blackened should not be hard or burnt it should be spotty with a bit of red showing.
Practice with the temperature.

Cornbread

This was from my restaurant The Cajun Attic and is literally world famous now.

Cream:
¾	cup	Margarine
1	cup	Sugar

Add and beat:
4		Eggs
1\2		Green pepper diced or spice it up with jalapeños
1	19 oz	can Creamed Corn
1	cup	Monterey Jack or mozzarella cheese shredded

Mix separately:
1	cup	Flour
1	cup	Cornmeal (course)
2	TBS.	Baking powder
1/2	tsp.	Salt

Add dry ingredients to the wet and beat until just mixed, do not overbeat, it will rise too high.

Pour into 9x13 pan and bake until golden brown on top about 1 hr. (Parchment on bottom helps)

Or make muffins, they take about 30min.

Coconut Shrimps

SPICE MIX:
1	cup	Flour
1	TBS.	Cayenne
1	TBS.	Sugar
1	TBS	Paprika
1	TBS.	Salt
½	tsp.	Thyme
½	tsp.	Onion powder
½	tsp.	Oregano
1	tsp.	Baking powder
½	tsp.	Garlic powder

BOIL SHRIMP: (about 3 per person) (I like shell on zipper backs 30/40 count works nicely)
In a crawfish boil: cayenne, onion, and lemon. Add shrimp to boiling boil and when the water boils again they are done.
Then shock in cold water and drain well.

COCONUT DIP:
IN THE BLENDER until smooth
1/2		Banana ripe
1	Cups	Cream10%
1 ½	TBS.	Curry powder

Add mixture to a roux and cook until thickened (back of spoon)
ROUX:
1	TBS.	Butter
1	tsp.	Flour

Methodology:
"And" this is where it gets vague.
Mix some beer and some of the flour/spice mix (thick back of spoon) to make a batter about the consistency of pancake batter or thinner. Now drink the rest of the beer.

First dust the cooked shrimp in the dry spice/flour mix and shake off, second dredge the shrimp through the beer batter.

Press both sides onto coconut you have put on a plate (shredded & sweet) both sides.
Be tidy here or you use a lot of coconut.

If the batter thickens open another beer to thin it as you go then drink the rest.

Heat about ½ inch of oil on med and fry both sides until golden brown or use a deep fryer if the batter falls off it is because the shrimp were probably too wet that's why they go through the dry/flour mixture.
So if this happens perhaps just open a bottle of wine and forget about them, you have had too many beers already.

Copyright

Onion Bhaji

Sift and mix:

100	gms.	Chickpea flour
1/4	tsp.	Chili powder
1/2	tsp.	Turmeric
1/2	tsp.	Baking powder
1/2	tsp.	Cumin

ADD

1	large	Onion sliced thin

ADD   Cold water until mixture is pasty and can form into a ball

Its pretty gooey but try to drop by the spoonful and Deep fry

It does not matter what they look like they taste great.

Pork Satay

Remove silver skin and trim fat from 1 pork tenderloin and slice lengthwise into long strips (about ¼" thick) marinate 2-24 hrs.

Marinade:

1	TBS	Soya sauce
1	TBS	Sugar
1	TBS	Lemon juice
1	TBS	Veg oil
1	tsp.	Black pepper
1	tsp.	Cumin
1	tsp.	Coriander
1	tsp.	Turmeric
1	tsp.	Fish sauce
1	tsp.	Chopped garlic

Peanut Sauce   (WORK IN PROGRESS)

In a bowl:

¼	cup	Smooth peanut butter
1	TBS	Rice wine vinegar
1	TBS	Fresh ginger (grated)
1	TBS	Soy Sauce
1	TBS	Vegetable oil
1	tsp.	Sesame oil
1	tsp.	Chili garlic sauce

ADD:
| ¼ | cup | Hot water and whisk until smooth. |

Or buy PC Memories of Szechwan (Canadians will know this one)

BBQ pork until cooked and enjoy with your other favorite Thai dish (Preferably one you can make)

Samosas

The Mukut Indian restaurant this is a clone

FILLING
In a sauce pan:

1	TBS	Vegetable oil
1	med	Onion diced fine
2	TBS	Garlic diced
2	tsp.	Curry powder
	Dash of	Salt and Pepper

Cook until soft then add:

1	med	Potato diced fine
1		Carrot diced fine

Cook until tender then add:

1	cup	Frozen peas

DOUGH
Mix:

2	Cups (225 Gms.)	Flour
2	tsp.	Salt
1/4	cup	Cold lard cut in
1/3	cup (80 ml)	Water

Knead and let stand for 30 min. Then fill and deep fry
I've been making mine in 5" rounds then folding over and seal edge with a fork.
(Kind of like an empanada) I have not yet mastered the triangular shape.

SAUCE
Mix:

2	TBS	Heaping of Mayonnaise
1		Green onion diced fine
1/2	tsp.	Green hamburger relish
1	tsp.	Chili garlic
1/2	tsp.	Chili powder
1	tsp.	Worchester sauce

Adjust thickness with milk
Make ahead and chill.

Spring Rolls

Major party favorite here

Filling: best to have all ingredients ready in front of you.
Soak in water 30 min then strain and chop fine.

1-½	oz.	Glass noodles
½	oz.	Black fungus dried

REMEMBER all ingredients are diced fine.
In wok or pot heat on high:

½	cup	Vegetable oil	
1	TBS	Garlic	
4	oz.	Chicken (breast)	Add shrimps too if you like

Lower heat and add:

	the	Glass noodles
	the	Black fungus
½	cup	Bamboo shoots
¼	cup	White cabbage shredded
1	sml	White onion
¼	cup	Carrot
¼	cup	Green onion
1	tsp.	Black pepper
1	TBS	Oyster sauce
1	TBS	Sugar
1	TBS	Soya sauce
1	tsp.	Fish sauce

When all is cooked, put in strainer and let sit for 20 min to allow the liquid to drain.
Use this time to make the Dipping sauce:
In a saucepan cook over med heat until thickened then cool.

Dipping sauce Boil:

1	cup	Sugar
1	cup	Rice wine vinegar
1	TBS	Chili garlic sauce
1	TBS	Sesame seeds
2	TBS	Soya sauce (dark)
1	tsp.	Garlic chopped
1	tsp.	Cornstarch

Fill:
Spring roll wraps. (Difficult to find, but they have them frozen in Asian food shops)

Mix a little flour and water to make a paste use this to glue the spring roll wraps. To fill lay the wrap with one of its points towards you. Place the filling on and fold the point over and pull in the stuffing to make it tight. Fold the side triangles in and roll to make the shape. Use the glue to seal the last tip of wrap.
Deep fry in   Vegetable oil until golden brown.

Smoked Salmon App

Beth the royalty check is in the mail

Slice diagonal
1/4 "   slices   French baguette bread

Slice thin as possible a small side of the best
                Smoked Salmon you can buy

The Sauce:

Whisk in the kitchen Aid:

150	grms	Cream cheese soft
150	grms	Mayonnaise

After smooth ADD:

1	TBS	Lemon juice to taste
1/2	tsp.	Salt and pepper
1/3	tsp.	Horseradish
1	tsp.	Red Onion diced fine
1	tsp.	Capers diced fine
1/2	tsp.	Juice from cappers

Salads and Dressings

Blender salad dressings:
I have only put a few in the book but once you have mastered the technique, the sky is the limit.
Here are the basic ratios

Oil to vinegar is 3 to 1
Adding water will help emulsify the dressing and reduce the tangy flavor.
Sugar too will cut the vinegar taste.

Montreal Vinaigrette Dressing

This is Cindy's fav

Blend in blender:

1/4	cup	Olive oil
1/2	cup	Veg oil
1/4	cup	Vinegar
3	TBS	Water
3	tsp.	Montreal Steak Spice
1	tsp.	Garlic chopped
1/2	tsp.	Sugar

Follow that Food

Greek Salad Dressing

See the trend here? (Duh its very similar to the Montreal dressing.)

In the blender:

1/4	cup	Olive oil
1/2	cup	Veg oil
1/4	cup	Red wine vinegar
1	TBS	Lemon juice (fresh squeezed)
3	TBS	Water
1/2	tsp.	Dijon mustard
1	tsp.	Garlic fresh
1	tsp.	Oregano
1/2	tsp.	Sugar
1/2	tsp.	Black pepper

If you find you would like it tangier add in a bit of white vinegar.

Mexican Salad Dressing

From my old "Hacienda Dos Gringos" Restaurant

In the blender:

1/4	cup	Vinegar
3	TBS	Water
1	TBS	Jalapeño peppers
1	tsp.	Garlic chopped
1	tsp.	Worchester sauce
1	tsp.	Gringo spice mix (see recipe under spice mixes)
1		Egg
1	cup	Veg oil

Back in the day we used to put all the ingredients into the blender, turn it on, then add the oil until we liked the thickness.

Ranch Salad Dressing

I include this one because it is the only creamy dressing I make

Blender:

1	tsp	Parsley fresh
½	tsp	Onion fresh
½	tsp	Onion powder
½	tsp	Garlic fresh
½	cup (125 ml)	Mayonnaise
1	Cup (125 ml)	Buttermilk

Thai Yum Salad Dressing

3	TBS	Lemon or lime juice
1	TBS	Garlic chopped
3	TBS	Fish sauce (Careful some brands are very strong, I like the brand called "Lucky")
1	TBS	Sugar

Optional

1	tsp.	Red chilies or more to make it spicy.

Shake well and serve on salad

To make a yum salad

On a platter arrange:

4-5	leaves Romaine lettuce chopped
4-5	Shrimps cooked
4-5	Tender Steak slices cooked
4-5	Cucumber slices
3-4	Lemon wedges

Garnish with: Carrot shredded
red pepper julienned
green onions sliced diagonally

Pour dressing over entire salad as evenly as possible.

Muffuletta Olive Salad

A New Orleans Specialty Sandwich

Or

Put it on anything especially home made Pizza

Chop in small pieces (about ¼" thick)

2	cups	Olives
3	stocks	Celery
2	cups	Cauliflower
3		Carrots
½	cup	Green peppers
½		Red onion in slivers
1/8	cup	Parsley chopped fine
1	cup	Olive oil extra virgin
¼	cup	Vinegar
2	TBS.	Garlic
1	TBS.	Basil
½	tsp.	Black Pepper
1	tsp.	Oregano
1	tsp.	Ginger
½	tsp.	Salt
½	cup	Veg oil

Let this mixture marinate and keep chilled in the refrigerator.

Now here's the thing:

Find yourself a nice fresh crusty roll or a sub
Cut to open lengthwise place a slice or 12 of ham, salami and cheese. Drizzle the olive salad over generously and eat over the sink.

My restaurant version was: Cajun Sausage slices, folded into a flour tortilla topped with Monterey Jack cheese, baked until done, slathered with the olive salad on top. Yummy

Mango Chicken Salad

Something to do with your left over "astronaut chicken"

(You know those rotisserie chickens in the bubble helmet package you get at the grocery store)

LIME DRESSING
Put in blender.

1/2	cup	Lime juice fresh
1/4	cup	Fish sauce (careful some brands are concentrated add to taste.)
2	TBS	Oil
1	TBS	Garlic
2	TBS	Sugar
1	TBS	Red-hot chilli flakes

SALAD:

1		Mango julienne
1		Carrot julienne
4 oz.		Snow peas blanched
1/4	cup	Mint or Thai basil chopped or both
1/2	cup	Cilantro chopped
1/4	cup	Green onions chopped
1/3	cup	Peanuts
2	TBS	Sesame seeds (toasted if you have time)
Diced		Astronaut chicken hahah

NOODLES:

Use rice noodles like Thai or Vietnamese vermicelli.
Pasta, or rice works too.
Depending on the size of bag I use about 2 cups cooked.
Follow the directions for cooking
Then rinse and chill or leave at room temperature
Now chop into 2" lengths

Add dressing and toss all ingredients in a bowl

Wing Ding Salad

One of our favorites at the Christmas meal Thanks for this one Cindy

Don't let the name fool you there are no wings in this salad, it's just a Cindyism.

Blanch in hot water
1	cup	Green beans cut in half

Add
1	can	Petit green peas (drained) Cindy uses Le Sur peas
4	stalks	Celery chopped
1		Red onion chopped
1		Green pepper chopped
1	sml jar	Pimentos chopped (or roast your own red peppers)
1	can	Hearts of palm/or Baby Corn or both

Dressing:
Add about an hour before serving, it kind of over marinates otherwise
3/4	cup	Sugar
1/4	cup	Veg oil
1/2	cup	Vinegar
1	TBS	Water
1	tsp.	Salt
dash		Paprika

Breads

What you really need to know about making bread are these basic principles
Measure carefully and record your method so when you find your dream loaf you can make it over and over. It takes a bit of practice. All-purpose flour will make a lighter bead than bread flour.

For:
4 cups (550 gms) Flour

Use 1 cup warm water and add.
1 TBS yeast
1 TBS Sweet (sugar or honey etc. to activate the yeast)
1 tsp Salt

The rest is up to you.
You can mix the flours, use molasses to make darker bread, add cheeses, Jalapeños, olives etc. etc. no limit to it, sprinkle the top with sesame seeds, Poppy seeds or your favorite whatever.

Most yeast breads rise twice, the first one to double it then punch it down and let the final rise shape your loaf. It also needs a warm place with no breeze, a proofing oven is about 100 degrees so you could slightly heat your own oven and turn it off during the rising.
Note all breads will rise given enough time (they will even rise in a fridge) so if it seems to be taking too long be patient.

You can cook it in a loaf pan or as a free shaped bread loaf.
If you make a bread like French loaf and it came out looking like a flat Panini you have a bit too much liquid but it will still taste good, perhaps you could just say "hey look I just made a Panini guys dig in"
If you have too much flour it will be heavy when cooked.

Practice, practice.
Just remember there are no bad breads…. Or is it no bad questions… I don't know there may be a lawyer in there somewhere.

Copyright

Country Style Bread

Mix:

1 ¼	cups (290 ml)	Warm water (120 degrees)
1	TBS	Yeast
3	TBS	Sugar
1	TBS	Olive oil

Mix

4	cups (550 gms)	Bread flour
1 ½	tsp	Salt

Knead wet and dry together until glutinous (about 3 min in the kitchen aid with dough hook)
Oil sides and rise for 40 min cover with damp cloth

Punch down put in loaf pan or shape French loaf and let the bread rise about 1 hr. until you like the size.
Brush with egg wash (room temperature) if you want a brown shine.

Place a water bath under bread while cooking if you want the crust softer and chewier.
Bake at 375 for 25 min until the top is the color you like.

Practice makes perfect, get to know the texture of the dough out of the kitchen aid and next time adjust the flour to suit your style.

Portuguese Bread

Mix
- 1 ¼ cup (290 ml.) Warm water (120 degrees)
- 1 TBS Honey
- 1 TBS Yeast

Mix dry then add water and honey
- 4 cups (550gms) Bread flour
- 1 ½ tsp. Salt

Knead wet and dry until glutinous (about 3 min in the kitchen aid)
Oil sides of the bowl and rise for 40 min covered with a warm damp cloth

Punch down
Shape into loaf or put in bread pan and let raise 1hr, or until you like the size.
Brush with egg wash (room temperature) if you want a brown shine.
You can add stuff to the top here too.

Bake at 375 for 25 min with a pan of water under the rack.

Whole Wheat Bread

Mix
1 ¼	cups	Water
1	TBS	Yeast
1	TBS	Sugar
2	TBS	Olive oil

Mix
2	cups (275)gms	Bread flour
2	cups (275)gms	Whole-wheat flour
1 ½	tsp.	Salt

Add liquid to dry and knead until glutinous (about 3 min in the kitchen aid)
Rise about an hour.

Punch down and shape into desired loaf or loaf pan
For a shine brush it with room temperature egg wash.

Bake at 375 for 25 min.

Corn Tortillas

I've been working on this one for a while and I like the results

Get your scale out

Mix:
240	gms	Masa flour mix (bit hard to find)
60	gms	Flour
30	gms	Corn meal (course grind)
1	tsp	Salt

Mix and add
1 ¼	Cups	Warm Water added slowly then adjust
1	TBS	Lime or lemon juice

Mix in kitchen aid

Knead with hands then let rest 30 min

In Tortilla press
25	gms	Balls make small size for tacos
40	gms	Balls make enchilada size

Flour Tortillas

Thanks for this one James

Mix in a bowl:

2 ¼	cups (300 gms)	White flour
½	tsp.	Baking powder
½	tsp.	Salt

Cut in like pastry

¼	cup	Butter (room temperature)
¾	cup	Water warm

Knead on a floured surface until smooth and elastic.
For 6" torts, make 8-10 balls (30gms) and cover with damp cloth for 20 min.

Roll out thin (this is the hard part) and cook in a hot dry pan until bubbles form and brown specks appear about 1 min.

Pizza Dough

Makes a medium size Thanks for this one Dana

Mix in a bowl for 10 min:

3/4	Cup	Warm water
1 1/4	tsp.	Yeast
1/4	tsp.	Brown sugar
1	TBS	Olive oil

Mix:

2 1/3	cups (224 gms)	Flour (all purpose)
1/2	tsp.	Salt

Adjust the thickness
Add wet to dry and knead (in the kitchen-aid dough hook)
Let proof until doubled for 1 hour or not it still makes a great pizza with no rise.
Punch down let rest for 10 min then make pizza.

Scones Coffeehouse

Mix:
1 ¾	cup (240 gms)	Flour
4	tsp.	Baking powder
1/8	tsp.	Salt
3	TBS	Sugar

Cut in:
5	TBS (70 gms)	Butter cold and in pieces

Add:
½	cup	Raisins or currants (optional)

Mix together:
¼	cup	Sour cream
2	TBS	Maple syrup (thanks for the syrup Earl)
¼	tsp.	Vanilla extract
½	cup	Milk

Overworking makes tough scones
Add liquid to flour all at once and mix gently with a fork until well blended. With floured hands make 2-3" (70grms) balls and place on baking sheet with parchment and flatten with your hands.

Make egg wash;
1	Egg
Splash	Milk

Brush on top then Bake at 400 for 10-15 min or until golden brown.

Red Lobster Biscuits

Ya ya prove I plagiarized it?

Combine in large bowl:
2	cups. (270 gms)	Flour
1	TBS	Baking powder
1	TBS	Sugar
1/2	tsp.	Kosher Salt
1/2	tsp.	Garlic powder
1/4	tsp.	Cayenne pepper

Add: and cut in
85	gms	Shortening

Mix: and add to flour until just moist
3/4	cup	Milk
1	TBS	Vinegar

Fold in:
1 1/2	cup	Cheddar cheese

Make biscuit size biscuits ha ha about 1/4 cup each
Bake in 450-degree oven for 15 min

Topping Whisk:
60	gms	Butter melted
1	tsp.	Parsley chopped
1/2	tsp.	Garlic powder

Brush each biscuit and serve immediately.

Soups

A how to do guide for all soups
This is a basic chicken stock recipe that gives you the initial quantities to make a great soup.
The rest is up to you, work with your fridge or use your favorites. However I have included some real winners.

To make chicken stock:
Start with a mirepoix which is carrots, celery and onion equal quantities that you decide on.
Sauté in a little veg oil then add the bones, fat, skin and water.
Now there are 2 schools of thought on the next part. Some say simmer slowly so your stock is clear. I say boil it hard to get all the flavor out of those old bones and I am convinced this way has more flavor albeit it's cloudy (bite me). You can add water as necessary and after a few tries you will get the hang of it.

I boil mine about 1-2 hours depending on amount of bones. Boil it down until it has a nice flavor then stop. You can refrigerate it until the fat comes to the top and hardens then skim it off, but I leave some for extra flavor.

The basic soup base:
Sauté: until clear

1	TBS	Butter or Olive oil
1		Onion chopped (size not too important here)
1	TBS	Garlic chopped

Add:

2	ltrs.	Chicken stock
1	TBS	Salt or less to taste

Bought Chicken stock has salt already so add to taste

Killer Chicken Noodle Soup

Homemade chicken soup cures everything.

Make soup base from previous page:

Add:

½	cup	Cooked chicken (or more)
3		Lasagna noodles (cooked and chopped up)
1		Carrot diced pre cooked
1	tsp.	Poultry seasoning
1	tsp.	Pepper
1	tsp.	Basil

Simmer until carrots are soft but not mushy.

Tortilla Soup

(One of my favorites)

Sauté: until clear
1	TBS	Butter or Olive oil
1		Onion chopped (size not too important here)
1	TBS	Garlic chopped

Add:
2	ltrs.	Chicken stock
1	TBS	Salt (or less to taste if using boxed chicken stock)

Now add:
½	cup	Mexican Tomato Salsa or Pico de Gallo (homemade if you have it) pg 56

To serve add to each bowl:
Some	Tortilla chips broken up slightly or in strips
Slices of	Avocado
A little	Cheese shredded

Follow that Food

Cream Soups

My basic cream soup
Cream of mushroom (or anything you want)

Sauté: until clear
1	TBS	Butter or Olive oil
1		Onion chopped (size not too important here)
1	TBS	Garlic chopped
2	cups	Mushrooms diced or sliced

Make a roux:
By adding:
2	TBS	Flour

Cook until slightly browned

Add:
1.5	ltr	Chicken stock
1	tsp.	Basil
1	TBS	Salt (less to taste. bought chicken stock has salt)
		Pepper to taste.

Cook on low until boiling
Add:
2	TBS	Flour stirred into cream
500	ml	Cream (5% 10% or even milk) but for Howard and Freddie whipping cream!!

Bring to almost a boil and simmer until flavors meld.
If you want a more intense mushroom flavor puree some of the mushrooms.
And it's better after you freeze it and reheat.

Brie Asparagus & Champagne

Yummy off the scale

Sauté until clear
1	TBS	Butter
½		Onion
½	TBS	Garlic

Add: bring to boil

1	Ltr	Chicken stock

Puree in:

200	gms	Brie Cheese skin and all (about a 4" round)

Season with salt and pepper

Gently add:
1	can	Asparagus in half inch lengths with juice (I know, I know it's a can but just suck it up, they're always available and works best with the juice)

At serving time
Pour in:
120	ml (4oz)	Champagne to taste. (Does not need to be Dom Perignon)

It should NOT taste like wine so please suggest an amount for me? I have never measured this part before.

Fish Chowder

Thanks Howard and Freddie.

Cut
3	Lbs. (1.3 kg.)	Fish fillets into ¾ " cubes

Sprinkle   Salt and Pepper

Cook for 5 min in
2	cups	Water

Remove fish to cool and reserve the stock

Fry
250	gms	Bacon and dice into ½ " pieces

Let it cool

Sauté in the stockpot
2	TBS	Butter
1	cup	Onion diced
1	cup	Celery diced
¼	cup	Carrots diced fine
1	med	Potato diced

Make a roux
Add
2	TBS	Flour

Cook until starting to brown

Add
1 ½	tsp	Tarragon
1	tsp	Thyme
		The stock
		The bacon

Bring to almost a boil

Add
500	mls	Whipping cream
2	cups	Fish stock you reserved

Stir until heated (do not boil)

You can thin it out to the consistency you like.

Serve each bowl with a pat of butter

Gumbo with Cajun Sausage

This is a tricky one and a bit dangerous so keep a lid handy for fire.

Cajun Roux; my way or the highway 61
Note: have all the ingredients at the ready; they get added quickly.

In a large sauce pan
Heat on high:

| ¾ | cup (200 ml) | Vegetable oil until it starts to smoke |

Carefully add:

| ¾ | cup (200 ml) | Flour using a long whisk (gloves are good here it steams heavily) |

Cook until a little darker than refried beans or peanut butter.

Now toss in:

2	stocks	Celery sliced
1	TBS	Garlic
½	cup	Onion diced

Reduce heat and cook until tender.

Add:

1	TBS	File gumbo (don't try to substitute, a bit hard to find)
1	tsp.	Cayenne pepper
1	tsp.	Black pepper
Dash of		Salt

Add

1 ¼	ltrs	Water
½	cup	Salsa
2		Cajun sausages cooked and sliced (or more)

Simmer until it thickens and adjust if necessary it should be twice as thick as gravy.

Serve over cooked rice, a very manly soup here.

Sauces

Here are some good ones.

Basic White Sauce

I use this in place of heavy whipping cream, more flavor and healthier.

Sauté:
1	squirt	Veg oil
1	cup	Onion
1	cup	Green peppers diced

Add:
1	ltr	Chicken stock
500	ml	Water

Simmer on low until peppers darken

Add:
750	ml	Cream 10%

Heat gently but don't boil.

I freeze mine in zip lock bags and use as needed

So any dish now becomes a "WOW" dish
like Big Mamou, enchiladas, quesadillas, pasta.
Even mac and cheese becomes gourmet.

Black Bean Salsa

Pairs nice with Caribbean pork pg. 75

Dice:
1	Lb. (454 gms)	Tomatoes ripe
1		Avocado
1/4	cup	Red onion diced

Add:
1/2	cup	Canned black beans rinsed (I freeze the remaining)
1/4	cup	Cilantro chopped
2	TBS	Lemon juice
1	TBS	Veg oil
1	TBS	Jalapeño peppers diced fine or pureed
1	tsp.	Garlic chopped
1/2	tsp.	Kosher salt

Goes on or in Mexican dishes
Fajitas
Fish
Or garnishing any plate you want to jazz up.

Creole Sauce

For the love of really spice, hot so Bite me, woosies

Spice Mix:

1/4	cup	Corn starch
2	TBS	Sugar
1 ¾	tsp.	Oregano
1	tsp.	White Pepper
1	tsp.	Paprika
1	tsp.	Black Pepper
1	tsp.	Basil
1	tsp.	Cayenne pepper
¼	tsp.	Salt

SAUTEE:

126	gms	Margarine or butter
1	TBS	Garlic heaping
3	cups	Onions chopped
1/2	bunch	Celery (that's all the stocks even the leaves)

ADD:

	ALL	The spice mix
1		Green pepper chopped into bite size
4	CUPS	Chicken stock
1/3	CUP	Louisiana hot sauce bottled
3		Bay leaves
56	OZ.	Tomatoes canned diced

Simmer on low until tender

Great with pasta
Mixed in rice
Spicy sausages.

I realize there is no real recipe for this sauce in my book, that's because I serve it like this.
Make a pilaf with warm rice in a shallow bowl, heat up the creole and make a moat.
Top with blackened shrimps.
Over the top good and this cans or freezes well.

Cajun Curry

Sauté:

1	TBS	Veg oil
1	TBS	Onion
2	TBS	Garlic chopped

add

1	cup	Chicken stock
1 ½	cups	Water

stir in

1/2	cup	Curry spice mix pg. 7

cook on low heat until thickened

yield approx. 3 cups should serve 4 people

To make the curry
Make rice (your favorite recipe)
add cubed cooked chicken or whatever to the curry sauce
Pour over rice then shredded jack or mozzarella cheese on top
Sprinkle with pecans
(Optional) shredded fried potato or even potato chips

Bake in individual casserole dishes for about 30 min

Enchilada Sauce

Sauté:
1	TBS	Veg oil
1	tsp.	Garlic chopped
½		Onion chopped
½	tsp.	Oregano
½	tsp.	Ginger powder
½	tsp.	Savory

Boil in a little water
1		Ancho pepper dried de-seeded (can not be made without this)

Puree when ancho is tender

Add:
2	28oz	Crushed tomatoes canned
2	28 oz	of Water

Simmer until done

Obviously it's for enchiladas and burritos But...
This makes a great pizza sauce too!

This cans or freezes well.

Garlic King Sauce

Best Shawarma sauce ever or on your sandwich

120	gms	Margarine (butter will get too hard in the fridge)
10	gms	Veg oil
70	gms	Garlic fresh about 2 bulbs
1	tsp.	Lemon juice
½	tsp.	Salt

Blend on high until well mixed and smooth

This sh*t can be used for sautéing as well

Mild Salsa

1	28oz	Diced tomatoes canned or fresh
½	cup	Onion chopped
2	TBS	Mild salsa spice mix pg 4

Picco de Gallo Salsa

Always keep this one available

1	28oz	Diced tomatoes canned or fresh
½	cup	Onion chopped
¼	cup	Cilantro chopped
2	TBS	Olive oil
2	TBS	Mild salsa spice mix Pg 4
2	TBS	Lemon juice
½	tsp.	Garlic chopped

Use with corn chips
Nachos
All Mexican food
Breakfast
Fajitas
You get the idea now right?

Stir Fry Sauce

Heat on med for about 30 seconds
1 ½	tsp	Sesame oil
½	tsp	Chopped garlic
1	tsp	Ginger shredded Tip, keep it frozen and grate frozen skin on.

Add
½	cup	Chicken stock
1	TBS	Brown sugar
1	tsp	Chili garlic sauce
½	tsp	Salt
¼	tsp	Pepper
1 ½	tsp	Lemon juice

Mix then add
1	TBS	White wine
1 ½	tsp	Corn starch

Heat until slightly thick then pour over your stir fry just before serve

Thai Dipping Sauce

Boil until it thickens

1	cup	Sugar
1	cup	Rice wine vinegar
1	tsp.	Cornstarch
1	tsp.	Garlic chopped
2	TBS	Soya sauce dark
2	TBS	Chili garlic sauce
1	TBS	Sesame seeds

OMG use this with spring rolls and any Asian dinner, they will be licking their fingers.

Tomato Sauce Authentic Italian

San Marzano canned tomatoes (DOP if you can afford them)
Squeeze thru a sieve to make puree and discard pulp

Coat bottom of pot with Olive oil

Sauté
1		Onion quartered
1		Carrot chopped
1	stock	Celery
1	tsp	Garlic chopped
1	tsp	Pepper black

Add tomato puree
1	handful	Basil fresh is best

Simmer for 2 hours.
Re-sieve out solids and your done

V-H Sauce

For Ribs and Chicken

¼	cup	molasses
1/3	cup	honey
4		cloves garlic chopped fine
¼	cup	Soya sauce
1/6		lemon squeezed
dash of		vinegar
		Salt
		Pepper
		Dry mustard
		Turmeric
		Thyme

Method:

For ribs remove silver skin from back of ribs
Put in baking dish and pour the sauce over ribs
Cook until the sauce bubbles and thickens about 1 hr. turning ribs every once in a while

Good for chicken wings too.

Side Dishes

Cajun BBQ Corn

Open corn and remove the silk
Soak for ½ hour

Make the Cajun Butter:

1	tsp.	Paprika
½	tsp.	Onion powder
½	tsp	Garlic powder
½	tsp.	Kosher salt
¼	tsp.	Thyme
¼	tsp.	Oregano
¼	tsp.	Cayenne
½	cup	Butter soft

Open the cornhusks, brush on Cajun butter
Close and tie with husk pieces or string.

BBQ for about 30 min turning frequently and don't worry when the husks burn.

Scalloped Potatoes

Dana says, "It makes a good Mac and Cheese" but I wonder about him

I say, "Quit messing with my recipes"

Grease an 8"X8" Baking dish

Layer:

3		large potatoes, peeled and thinly sliced
1/2	cup	Onion chopped

In a saucepan make a roux:

2	TBS	Butter
2	TBS	Flour

Gradually add:

1 1/4	cup	Chicken broth
1	TBS	Mayonnaise
1/2	tsp.	Salt
1/4	tsp.	Pepper

Sprinkle with:

Paprika

Cover and bake at 325 for about 2 hours until tender

Dad's Favorite Potatoes

Boil:
3	cups	Chicken stock or enough to cover them
4	med	Potatoes cubed

Drain and mash with:
2	TBS	Butter
	Splash of	Milk

Stir in:
2		Green onions
½		Green pepper (red if its Christmas)
1 ½	cups	Cheddar cheese or other fav.

Place in casserole and bake until hot and edges are crispy.

Olive Oil Roasted Spuds

In a large bowl:

4		Potatoes (skin on) diced about 1"
1/3	cup	Olive oil
1	TBS	Basil dried
1	TBS	Oregano
		Salt and pepper to taste

Place on shallow tray and sprinkle generously with:
Parmesan cheese grated

Bake at 425 until soft inside and crispy outside about 20 min.

Carrots Flambéed in Tequila

A real flavor changer and not your old boring carrots

Par boil al dente:
3-4   Carrots

Toss in a skillet and add:
3   TBS   Butter

Bring up to very hot and toss in:
1   oz.   Tequila

Light with flame immediately and stand back (a BBQ lighter works best) When flame goes out serve immediately.

Even if tequila brings back bad memories you will love these.

Tabbouleh

Authentic Lebanese Side Dish

Soak: for 20 min
2-3   TBS   Bulgur (wheat germ)
Rinse and let stand for 10 min.

Mix:
3   bunches   Parsley finely chopped
1   cup   Mint fresh chopped
1   Tomato chopped
½   Onion chopped
½   cup   Olive oil
¼   cup   Lemon juice fresh
                         Salt and Pepper to taste
Toss in the bulgur here

½   tsp.   Cayenne pepper (optional)

It is also very good as a topping on a house salad

Main Meals

Beef Chili

Bake in oven for 1 ½ hrs. or cook on stovetop
2.5   kg   Ground beef

In a large pot add
The cooked ground beef mashed....duh!
8   cups   Water
1   can   Tomato paste (I can't remember the size... it's the little one)
½   cup   Hot salsa (jalapeños)
1   cup   Chili powder
1   cup   Cumin
1/3   cup   onion flakes
1   TBS   Paprika
1   TBS   Salt
1   TBS   Sugar
1   TBS   Garlic powder
1   TBS   Cayenne pepper
1   19oz   Can kidney beans
1   29oz   Can crushed tomatoes

Simmer on low for at least 1 hr.
For tastier chili freeze then re-heat, everybody knows its always better this way

Vegetable Chili

Thanks for that one Sue Vallillee

Sauté:
2	TBS.	Garlic heaping and chopped
2	TBS	Vegetable oil
2		Bay leaves
1	TBS.	Oregano
1	TBS.	Red chili flakes
1	TBS.	Paprika
2	TBS.	Chili powder

Add to pot

2	cups	Carrots diced
1	cups	Turnips diced
2	28oz.	can Diced tomatoes
1	28oz.	can Tomato juice

Simmer until tender

After cooked add to pot:
2	cups	Green peppers chopped
2	28oz. can	Kidney beans (not drained)
1	28oz. can	Chick peas (drained)

You should definitely eat this with corn bread pg. 15
And it's a great base for jambalaya

This is how we did it in the restaurant:
1 scoop (6 oz.) of veg chili
½ scoop enchilada sauce
2 TBS meat or whatever
mix then in a single casserole dish lay rice on the bottom, pour the chili, top with Jack cheese, bake until hot and serve with corn bread.

Martha's Chili Rellenos

One more from the awesome chef Martha

Roast:
8		Poblano chili peppers (a bit hard to find but very important)

Place in paper or plastic bay to rest for ½ hour

FILLING:
Fry in skillet and drain:
225	gms	Pork ground
225	gms	Beef ground

Add:
1	medium	Onion chopped
1	clove	Garlic chopped
		Salt and pepper to taste
1	tsp.	Marjoram
½	cup	Tomatoes (canned)
1	TBS	Almonds (skinned and chopped)

Clean the chilies then slit them and carefully remove the seeds.
Stuff with the filling.

Whisk until stiff;
3		Egg whites

Then fold in:
3		Egg yokes

Dust the chilies with flour then cover with egg mixture

Fry in ¼ " veg oil until golden.

Heat:
1	cup	Enchilada sauce pg.54

Puddle on plate under chilies

SPINACH AND CHEESE VERSION

Substitute for the meat:
- Spinach cooked
- Monterey jack cheese

Beef Thai Basil

Thank's Bart Bristow for perfecting this one.

Best to have all the ingredients pre cut for speed

In a wok:
5	TBS	Veg oil heated until almost smoking

Cook for 1 min
1	tsp.	Garlic
4		Hot chilies or to taste

Sauté:
½		Onion chopped
¾	cup	Mushrooms chopped
1		Red Pepper chopped

Add:
1	lb.	Flank steak sliced in strips (or filet mignon)

Cook for 2 minutes

Mix and add:
½	tsp	Cornstarch
1	tsp	Sugar
1	TBS	Soya sauce
1	TBS	Fish sauce
1	TBS	Oyster sauce
3	TBS	Water

Toss in:
20	or more	Basil leaves

Serve with rice

Beef Korma

Marinate for at least 2 hrs.

700	gms.	Hamburger
½	cup	Yogurt plain

Add:

1	tsp	Salt

Cook over low heat until done and tender

Sauté

1	TBS	Olive oil
1		Onion chopped
Add and cook		Marinated burger

Add:

2	TBS	Curry powder
1	tsp	Turmeric
1	tsp	Garlic chopped
½	tsp	Chili powder
1	cup	Tomatoes (canned diced)
¾	cup	Frozen peas

Cook on low to med until hot and serve, usually with basmati rice.

Butter Chicken

Thanks for this one Darcy

Oven at 375

Cube:
1	lb (454 gms)	Chicken breast

Toss in veg oil and coat with Garam Tandoori powder and bake in 375 oven until done. Parchment paper is a good idea here.

Sauté:
2	TBS	Butter
½		Onion
2	tsp	Garlic chopped

Add:
½	cup (225 gms)	Butter
1	cup (240 ml)	Tomato sauce
2	cups	Cream 10%
1	tsp	Salt
1	tsp	Cayenne pepper
1	tsp	Garam Masala

Simmer 30 min then add chicken and serve with rice.

Caribbean Pork Tenderloin

2 pork tenderloins (trim fat and remove silver skin)

Pairs nice with Black Bean Salsa pg.51

Marinate pork 2- 4 hrs.

¼	cup	Lime juice
1	TBS	Lime zest
2	TBS	Olive oil
2	TBS	Onion minced
1	TBS	Ginger grated
1	TBS	Garlic chopped
1	TBS	Jalapeño pepper

Remove pork from marinade and wipe dryish (discard marinade)

Spice Rub:

1	TBS	Kosher salt
2	tsp	Curry powder
2	tsp	Coriander ground
1	tsp	Allspice ground
1	tsp	Black pepper
½	tsp	Nutmeg
½	tap	Cumin

Rub the spice on meat.

BBQ until done and don't overcook your pork eh!

Chicken on a Stick

For the paste:
- 1 tsp. Garlic powder
- 1 tsp. Onion powder
- 1 tsp. Paprika
- 1 tsp. Cumin
- 1/2 tsp. Basil
- 1/2 tsp. Thyme
- 1/2 tsp. Salt
- 1/4 tsp. Black pepper
- 1/8 tsp. Cayenne pepper

- 1/4 cup Veg oil

Rinse chicken in water, pat dry and marinate in paste for 30 to 60 min BBQ in cubes on a skewer or whole boneless skinless breasts.

Chicken Big Mamou

Was our signature dish from the Cajun Attic Restaurant

This one's a 2 pager (With boneless chicken breasts serves 4)

Dumpling spice mix			Mamou spice mix		
½	tsp.	Salt	1 ½	tsp.	Paprika
½	tsp.	Dry mustard	1	tsp.	Sage
½	tsp.	Cayenne	1	tsp.	White pepper
1/3	tsp.	Thyme	1	tsp.	Onion powder
¼	tsp.	Nutmeg	1	tsp.	Garlic powder
¼	tsp.	Baking powder	1	tsp.	Cayenne pepper
			1	tsp.	Basil
			½	tsp.	Black pepper
			½	tsp.	Thyme
			½	tsp.	Salt

Both of these spice mixes can be saved for the next time (oh don't worry there will be a next time)

Dumplings:
Whisk:

1		Egg
1	TBS	Onion (diced small) until frothy

Add:

1	TBS	Dumpling spice mix
2	TBS	Milk or cream 5% or better
½	cup	Flour add slowly

If it turns into an unmanageable sticky glob its just right.
Boil some water then drop spoon globs of the goo in and cook till done they don't look so good but no worries they taste great in the sauce later. If they look too big just cut them up. If the dumplings don't turn out … toss them they are not mandatory for the main event.   Bite me.

White sauce

Sauté:

1	TBS	Butter
1	TBS	Diced onion diced fine
1	TBS	Diced green pepper

add

1	cup	Chicken stock
½	cup	Water
¾	cup	Cream 10% or better

Cook on low until peppers soften and look dark

The Chicken:
In a saucepan melt 2 TBS of butter
Coat the 4 chicken breasts lightly with the Mamou spice mix (the more you put on the spicier it will taste)
It is easier to sprinkle one side then place spice side down in the pan then sprinkle the other side. Cook the chicken in the butter until it is done

Methodology:
How do I say this … the temperature is everything with this dish (somewhere between low and medium) the chicken should be boiling in the butter not frying and not simmering. If the temperature is too low the sauce will be on the white side and if the temperature is too hot the sauce will be very dark and bitter. You know the temperature is right when the butter and coating are caramelizing but not burning. Boy what could be easier eh?

Push the chicken aside in the pan and make a roux with 2 more TBS flour
Turn to high and deglaze with white wine (don't forget to have a glass to, you need it if you got this far)
Add the white sauce and the dumplings and cook for another few minutes on high then turn to low and it will remain in stasis well. This will give you time to do the veggies or whatever you decide will accompany the dish.
The finished sauce should be about the color of peanut butter however lighter or darker it will taste just as good.

To quote Cindy "ain't cooking great when you're not doing it?"
Ta Da!....
Enjoy ………….

Total preparation time is about 1 ½ hrs.

Red Chicken Curry

My interpretation from the Coriander Thai restaurant

Sauté:
2	TBS	Veg oil
1	tsp.	Red curry paste (Caution this can be very strong I use Thai Kitchen brand)

Add:
1-2		Chicken breasts diced or julienned

When half cooked add:
½	cup	Coconut milk

boil this until the oil comes to the top

Add:
2	TBS	Basil
2	TBS	Sugar
½	tsp.	Ginger grated
3		Kaffir lime leafs (optional or a squirt of lime juice)
¼	cup	Peanuts ground fine
½	cup	Coconut milk

Bring back to boil and serve with jasmine rice if you have it.

Cajun Dirty Rice

Alana's recipe won the cook off contest at the Cajun Attic Restaurant

Cook and set aside
1	cup	Rice

in
1.5	cups	Chicken stock

In the meat grinder:
100	gms	Chicken hearts and gizzards
60	gms	Chicken liver
70	gms	Ground beef

In a bowl mix:
1	tsp	Cumin
1	tsp	Paprika
¾	tsp.	Cayenne pepper
½	tsp	Thyme
¼	tsp	Mustard powder

In a pan
2	TBS	Veg oil
2	TBS	Butter

Cook meats and spices together then set aside

Sauté and set aside
1	stock	Celery
½	cup	Onion chopped fine
1/3		Green pepper chopped fine

Now mix everything together with
½	cup	Parsley chopped fine

Re-heat in oven if not hot enough

Fiesta Chicken

Mix:
2	cups	Flour
1	cup	Corn meal (course grind)
1	tsp	Salt
1	tsp	Black pepper
1	TBS	Oregano
1/4	cup	Sesame seeds

Egg wash
2		Eggs
1	TBS	Milk
dash		Veg oil

Half and flatten out
4		Chicken breasts

Add:
1	TBS	Green chilies
1	TBS	Cheese (Monterey jack is good)

Roll up as tight as possible

Dip in egg wash and roll in flour mix
Re-dip in egg wash and roll in flour mixture again.

Little trick here I found, is if you make them all then store them for a while in the fridge covered with the rest of the flour mix they hold their shape and fry nicer.

Deep fry both sides in enough veg oil to half submerse at 350 until golden brown.

Sprinkle with   Salsa
                 Cheese shredded

Bake in oven about 5 – 10 min until cheese melts.

Fried Chicken Quepos

A Costa Rican inspiration

4	cups	Corn flakes crushed to make about 1 cup
½	cup	Flour
1	TBS	Cayenne pepper or more
1	tsp.	Salt
1	tsp.	Garlic powder
1	tsp.	Black pepper
1	tsp.	Thyme

For a spicier chicken I like to dash Louisiana sauce on the chicken before I roll in the coating

Mix spices coat chicken and deep-fry until done

.

Fish Fry Batter

Crow Lake Style

1	TBS	Semolina flour
3	TBS	Heaping Cornmeal (course grind)
3	TBS	Flour heaping
1 ½	TBS	Whole wheat flour
1	tsp.	Salt
1	tsp.	Pepper
1/2	tsp.	Garlic powder
1/2	tsp.	Onion powder
1/2	tsp.	Baking soda
1/2	tsp.	Lemon pepper
1 ½	tsp.	Cayenne pepper

Make an egg wash with 1 or 2 eggs and a bit of water (or beer). Whisk until mixed.

Dredge fish in egg wash and then cover or roll in dry batter mix Fry in oil at 350 degrees until it floats and turns golden brown.

This coating can be used for any deep fried food.
Enjoy

Fish Fillets Thai

Thai sauce
Combine and reserve:

1	tsp.	Chili garlic sauce
2	TBS	Red pepper diced very fine
2	TBS	Onion diced very fine
1	TBS	Cilantro chopped fine
2	TBS	Lemon juice diced fine (ha ha got ya)
3	TBS	Soya sauce
1	TBS	Veg oil

Fry in oil;

500	gms	Fish filets your favorite kind

Transfer to serving plate and dress with spoonfuls of sauce.
Serve with rice.

Garlic Peppered Pork

Thanks for this one Bart Bristow

Trim silver skin from pork tenderloin:

Rub:

		Olive Oil to coat meat
2	TBS	Garlic chopped rub over entire surface
3	TBS	Black pepper rub over entire surface

Wrap in plastic and refrigerate as long as you have up to 8 hrs.

Cook in 450 degree oven until pink in middle, about 40 min

Pssst I use my $19 digital meat probe from Walmart with alarm and I never over cook meat now

Chicken Big Mamou Pasta

For 2

Pre cook:

150	gms	Pasta (al dente) then shock in cold water and coat lightly in veg oil
I use		fettuccini.

Use my basic white sauce pg.# 50 or use this one, you need about 1 cup per serving.

Sauté:

1	TBS	Butter
1	TBS	Diced onion diced fine
1	TBS	Diced green pepper

add

1	cup	Chicken stock
½	cup	Water
¾	cup	Cream 10% or better

Cook on low until peppers soften and look dark
set aside.

Methodology; sprinkle 2 chicken breasts with Mamou spice mix. Pg 7

2	TBS	Butter to skillet don't be shy with the butter.
2		Breasts of chicken

(How do I say this ... the temperature is everything with this dish (somewhere between low and medium) the chicken should be boiling in the butter not frying and not simmering. If the temperature is too low the sauce will be on the white side and if the temperature is too hot the sauce will be dark and bitter.)
Cook until chicken is done turning over regular, and then remove from pan and cube it.

Finish the dish
Make a roux in the pan you cooked the chicken

1 ½	TBS.	Flour
Deglaze	with	White wine

Add:

2	cups	White sauce not more wine... bite me

then add the precooked pasta (it will finish in the sauce)
Serve with the cubed chicken on top.

Martha's Thai Chicken

Thanks for this one my darling chef Martha

Serves 2

For the gravy (her words) Translated from Spanish

2	cloves	Garlic chopped
2	inches	Ginger shredded
¾	cup	Chicken broth
¼	cup	Soy sauce
1	tsp.	Sugar
1	TBS	Rice wine vinegar
2	TBS	Cornstarch

To prepare the dish

Sauté in butter and olive oil:
1	tsp.	Red curry paste (or to taste)
2	breasts	Chicken diced

When cooked add:
All	The gravy... sauce ha ha bite me

Bring up to hot then

Just before serving adjust the thickness
Add:
6		Green grapes halved
2	TBS	Cilantro fresh and chopped

Serve over jasmine rice

Meatballs

These are really good ones

500	gms	Ground beef (best if you make your own see pg 106)
¾	cup	Rolled oats
1		Egg
1	tsp.	Chilli powder
1	tsp.	Salt
½	tsp.	Garlic powder
¼	tsp.	Pepper

Combine all and knead until smooth, brown in pan and use for your favourite recipe Even better I bake mine on parchment for 15 min.

Fried Yardbird

Definitely the best you have ever had Southern Fried Chicken

THE CHICKEN
Combine

1/2	cup	Kosher salt
4	cups	Water
4		chicken thighs, bone in, skin on
4		chicken drumsticks, bone in, skin on

(Or chop up a whole chicken)
Refrigerate for 1-2 hours
Rinse and pat dry

THE MARINADE
Combine in a sealable plastic bag, and let marinate in the refrigerator overnight or 12 hours.

2	cups	Buttermilk
1/3	cup	Coconut milk
1	tsp.	Garlic minced

CHICKEN SHAKE
Combine in a mixing bowl and stir until blended.
Makes about ¾ cup. Save for next time …. Oh there will be a next time.

¼	cup	Paprika
1	TBS	Cumin
1	TBS	Black pepper
1	tsp.	Ginger
3	tsp.	Cayenne pepper
¼	tsp.	Cloves
½	tsp.	Cinnamon
1	tsp.	Garlic
2	tsp.	Celery salt
2	tsp.	Kosher salt

THE BREADING
Remove chicken from marinade, and discard (no not the chicken), allowing excess to drip off. Roll chicken in breading and shake off excess

1	cup	Flour
3	TBS	Semolina flour
2	TBS	Cornstarch
2	tsp.	Chicken Shake

Deep fry until cooked and let rest for 10 min.
Season with extra Chicken Shake to taste.

Greek Garlic Chicken

Marinade:

1/2	cup	Parsley fresh chopped
1/4	cup	White wine (dry)
1/4	cup	Olive oil
2	TBS	Lemon juice
1	TBS	Garlic minced
1	TBS	Black olive tapenade (buy it or make it)
1	tsp.	Oregano
1	tsp	Paprika
1/2	tsp	Kosher salt
1/4	tsp	Black pepper

Marinate chicken thighs for 4-6 hours
On the BBQ
Drain and boil the marinade for 1 min use to baste the chicken near the end of grilling time.

Ham Steaks

With Jack Daniels Mop

The mop:
½	cup	Jack Daniels
½	cup	Brown sugar
2	TBS	Dijon mustard
2	TBS	Corn syrup

Use a smoked cooked ham and you really only need to cook them to heat through and make the grill marks.

Mop the steaks frequently as you grill them.

Jamaican Jerk Lamb Shanks

Or pork shanks

Spice Mix:

1	TBS	Sugar
1	TBS	Onion dried minced
1	TBS	Salt
1	tsp.	Cayenne pepper
1	tsp.	Cinnamon
1	tsp.	Nutmeg
1	tsp.	Allspice
2	tsp.	Thyme

Method:
In a hot skillet sear the meat in oil then
Slit the meat and rub in chopped garlic
Coat the shanks with the spice mix
Individually wrap tightly in tin foil

Cook at 350 degrees for 1-2 hours on a cookie sheet depending on their size
Peel tin foil off carefully

Also very good with pork shanks

Serve with other stuff like veggies and potatoes or rice.

Lasagna a la Cindy

Thanks Aunt Shirley

Cindy has been claiming this one for years then served it to Aunt Shirley only to find out it was hers!

Cook:
8		Lasagna noodle al dente (set aside)
		Not oven ready they SUCK

Pan fry:
500	gms	Ground beef lean (drain off fat)

add:
1		Onion diced
½		Green or red pepper diced

Cook until soft

Add:
6		Mushrooms sliced
1	cup	Plain spaghetti tomato sauce
5	oz.	Tomato paste

Add:
1	tsp.	Oregano to taste
		Red chili flakes to taste
¼	tsp.	Celery salt
3	forkfuls	Hot banana pepper rings
		Salt and pepper to taste

Simmer 30 min

In a 9X12 oven dish
Place 4 noodles on bottom
Spread half the meat mixture
Spread half of both cheeses
Repeat

500	gms	Mozzarella cheese shredded
500	gms	Cottage cheese

Cover with tin foil and cook for 15 min. remove, cool and refrigerate.
To eat cook again 30 –40 min. remove tin foil for last 15 min.

Lemon Chicken

One better than Golden Palace Restaurant

Sauce:
1	cup	Sugar
1	cup	Rosas lime cordial
½		Lemon squeezed
1	TBS	cornstarch
a few drops		yellow food colouring is optional (not too much or it will look like dish soap)

Cook over med heat until thickened

Cover:
4	Chicken breasts skinless
with	Corn starch (enough to coat completely)

Boil:
In	Veg oil about 6 min

Drain and cool:

Re-coat   Chicken breasts in cornstarch

Cook again on high until golden brown

Julienne the cooked chicken breast and pour the sauce over

Serve with slices of lemon garnish.

Mac and Cheese

Every now and then you get it perfect

No KD will darken my door, but this is the adult version kiddies…. Bite me

Boil: in water with a little oil and salt
1-½ cups Elbow Macaroni until tender and rinse well

Sauté in a saucepan
1 TBS Margarine
¼ cup Onion chopped

Stir in
1 TBS Flour and cook gently, do not brown

Add
1 cup Milk and cook until bubbly and slightly thick

Stir in
2 cups (180 gms) Cheese shredded (your favorite kind Cheddar, Swiss etc.)
½ cup Tomatoes diced (canned or fresh)

Mix in cooked macaroni and put in casserole bake until crispy on top
I like to sprinkle poppy seeds on top before cooking.

Manicotti

Boil: 6-8 Manicotti shells about 6 min al dente in water

Pinch		Salt
1	TBS	Oil

Cook:

500	gms	Hamburger
1	med	Onion

Mix: along with the cooled hamburger

3		Green onions chopped
500	ml	Ricotta cheese
250	ml	Mozzarella cheese shredded
125	ml	Parmesan cheese shredded
1		Egg

Stuff Manicotti shells

Mix:

750	ml	Tomato sauce (your favorite)
250	ml	Water

Pour half into bottom of 9x13 baking dish

Place manicotti and pour remaining sauce over.
Bake in oven until cooked and bubbly on edges.

Peking Duck and Pancakes

Weird to include this one, but so worth doing

Slow cook ducks until tender??? Wild or domestic are different 5 hrs. to whatever. Remove skin and crisp it up in a frying pan with olive oil.

Pancakes
Mix and knead until smooth
1	cup	Flour
¾	cup	Boiling water

Roll out to about 5 inches
Brush with sesame oil (sparingly) and fry in hot skillet about 1 min per side then keep warm

Shred duck, add mix with the crispy skin and serve with:
- Green onions slivered
- Hoisin Sauce

Pecan Crusted Pork Tenderloin

Cut pork tenderloin in 1" slices and flatten with your hand.
Season with salt and pepper.

Dredge pork slices in maple syrup
Press into pecans (finely diced)
In a frying pan
2   TBS   Olive oil to skillet
                           pork with pecans
Cook pork for 3-4 minutes per side.

Set aside cooked pork medallions

Mix and add to skillet:
2   Oranges (juice only)
1   TBS   Maple syrup
1/2   tsp.   Cayenne pepper
1/2   tsp.   Cumin
Reduce unil slightly thick and pour over medallions.

Garnish with a few orange wedges.

Salmon Dave's Pasta

Thanks for this one David and for teaching me how to smoke salmon.

Precook 4 portions of fettuccini pasta (280 gms) al dente, stop in cold water and coat lightly in veg oil set aside.
Slice thin the best-smoked salmon you can buy
About 7 slices / person but more is better because you can nibble.

The sauce
Sauté:

1	TBS	Veg oil
1	tsp	Garlic chopped
1/3	cup	Onions chopped
1	stock	Celery chopped
1/4	cup	Green pepper chopped
1	TBS	Louisiana hot sauce or Tabasco
1 1/2	cup	Chicken stock
1 1/4	cup	Tomatoes diced
1/3	cup	Water
1	cup	Cream 10%

Add a dash of each spice:
- Oregano
- Paprika
- Basil
- Black pepper
- Cayenne pepper
- Sugar

The finish; Make a roux;

1	TBS	Veg oil
1	TBS	Butter
1	tsp	Garlic
4	TBS	Flour

A splash of white wine, put the rest of the bottle on the dinner table as if…

Add sauce and bring to temperature then add the drained pasta
(I recommend Fettuccini)

Adjust the thickness with white wine. Should be back of spoon.
Roll the sliced salmon in flowerets and arrange on top

Sprinkle on top — Black caviar (or Capers if your too cheap or you don't have any caviar)

Spaghetti with Italian Sausage and Spinach

For 2 people - NOT your typical "red sauce" ho-hum spaghetti!

Cook al dente in water:
140	gms	Spaghetti
1	tsp.	Salt
1	tsp.	Red chilies

Rinse and set

In a saucepan
Sauté:
1/3	cup	Olive oil
1	tsp.	Garlic
1/2		Yellow or green pepper
3		Mushrooms
4		Black Olives (pitted and halved)
1/2		Onion chopped coarse
2		Italian sausage sliced (best to cook first and then slice)

When sausage is cooked

Toss in:
½	cup	Chicken stock
Big handful		Spinach
The cooked		Spaghetti

When spinach is wilted serve
Sprinkle grated Asiago cheese on top

Spanakopita

Sauté
1 ½	TBS	Olive oil
1		Onion chopped
3		Green onions chopped
1	TBS	Garlic chopped

Mix together
2		Eggs lightly beaten
3-4	cups	Spinach
1/2	cup	Ricotta cheese
1	cup	Feta crumbled

Add to sauté and remove when spinach wilts

Melt:
½	cup	Butter

Brush on:
6	sheets	Phylo pastry

Put spinach filling in the phylo and fold or roll
Bake at 450 about 30 min until golden brown (best if cooked on parchment paper)

Spinach Quesadillas

Or asparagus when they are in season

Béchamel Sauce:

Sauté
3	TBS.	Butter
3	TBS	Flour

Add
2 ½	cups	Milk
1	tsp.	Salt

Heat until thickened and firm enough to stay on top of tortilla. Thin with milk if needed.

Wilt:
2	TBS	Onions
2		Mushrooms
1	cup	Spinach
Add:	a dash	Worchester sauce

Fill flour tort with spinach mixture

Add: Cheese Monterey Jack shredded

Roll up or fold in half
Cover entire tortilla in sauce (so it will not become toast)
Sprinkle cheese on top bake in oven 375 about 10 min until the edges darken a bit

Serve with Picco de Gallo salsa if you like

Tacos el Pastor

Inspired by the Taco Brown Taqueria in Puerto Escondido Mexico

Marinade 4 to 24 hours

450	gms	Pork tenderloin (cleaned and sliced in ½" rounds)
1	cup (250 ml)	Pineapple shredded or tidbits canned or fresh, drained
1		Onion chopped fine
¼	cup	Cilantro chopped
1	TBS	Chili powder
1	tsp.	Cumin
1	tsp.	Oregano
1	tsp.	Pepper
1	tsp.	Garlic chopped fine
¾	tsp.	Salt

Heat:

2	TBS	Olive oil

Pan fry with the marinade until cooked then dice fine.

To be real authentico make my homemade corn tortillas in 3-4 inch rounds

Off the scale good
CORN TORTILLAS

Mix:

240	gms	Masa flour mix
60	gms	Flour
30	gms	Corn meal (course)
1	tsp	Salt
1 ¼	Cups	Warm water added slowly put the lemon in the water
1	TBS	Lime or lemon juice

Mix in Kitchen Aid with dough hook

Knead with hands then let rest 30 min

In Tortilla press

25	gms	Rolled into a ball will make small tacos

Cook on high heat in a skillet until done but soft and set-aside
To serve
Heat the Al Pastor in a skillet with a little cheese on top
Heat the tortillas in another skillet combine and serve with salsa and hot sauce.

Venison Meatloaf

Thanks for this one Brigadier General Carl.

And I quote:

"This is a dish to be cooked by men who don't know how to cook to feed to women who say they don't like venison." The most stupid male can't go wrong in cooking it, and the female who yammers the loudest about her dislike for venison will rave over it. Proportions don't matter much.

Sauté

1		small Onion chopped
½		Green pepper chopped
1	clove	Garlic diced fine

In a bowl mix thoroughly

450	gms	Venison ground
115	gms	Pork ground
½	cup	Milk or catsup or Chilli or tomatoes or sour cream or any combination thereof
1	stalk	Celery diced or carrot diced *doesn't matter*
3	TBS	Parsley chopped
½	tsp.	Black pepper
Pinch		Thyme and basil

Place in loaf baking pan and sprinkle liberally with paprika then Bake for about 40 minutes

Sausages

I included these because they are fun to make and really, who doesn't like sausages eh really??

You can buy a meat grinder for like $50 or (ask for it as a birthday present)
And a sausage stuffer for about $80 (Highly recommend this because it makes it enjoyable and 10 times faster) then ask for this one at Christmas, heh heh!
You can buy sausage casing at any butcher.

That's all the equipment you need, well….maybe some friends and beer too.

Once you buy your grinder you can start making all kinds of stuff.
Ground hamburger, I make mine out of top sirloin and filet mignon fat trimmings, prime rib makes a nice hamburger too.
You will never go back to grocery store hamburger again.

You can also make
Ground pork
Ground chicken
Ground onion
Etc.

Note: when cutting meat for grinding cut into long strips not cubes, they will go through the grinder much easier.

Cajun Sausage

SPICE MIX: (makes 6 batches about 4 lbs. each)

45	gms	Black pepper
42	gms	Cayenne pepper
13	gms	Red chilies
11	gms	Basil
<u>106</u>	gms	Salt

217 gms in total

If you have a meat grinder use the fine or medium disk.
You can grind the onion, garlic and jalapeño too.
Makes about 4 lbs.

In the Kitchen Aid mix well:

1500	gms.	Ground pork
70	gms	Jalapeño
235	gms	Onion (pureed)
20	gms	Garlic (chopped)
35	gms	Spice mix
150	ml.	Ice water

Now put in casings with middle size tube. Or you can just make patties; the taste is all there.
Freeze uncooked.

FYI: types of pork cuts
- PICNIC ROAST — 30% FAT (best)
- SHOULDER — 20% FAT
- BUTT — 20% Fat
- BACON — 40% (if more fat needed)

Bratwurst Sausage

Thanks for this one Google.

Spice mix:

1	TBS	Kosher salt
1	TBS	Marjoram
2	tsp	Caraway seeds
3	tsp	Pepper black
1	tsp	Allspice

Mix in the Kitchen Aid

1000	gms	Pork shoulder or butt
500	gms	Ground veal
		The spice mix
50	gms	Bacon
60	ml	Ice water
1	TBS	Garlic (optional)

Italian Sausage Mild

Spice mix:

2	TBS	Paprika
2	TBS	Italian parsley leaves chopped
1	TBS	Salt
1	TBS	Black pepper
1 ½	tsp.	Fennel seeds
1	tsp.	Cayenne
½	tsp.	Anise ground

Grind medium disk:
1.4	kg.	Boneless pork butt well marbled

(not enough fat? substitute 1 lb. with bacon)

Mix in the Kitchen Aid

		The ground pork
		The spice mix
2	TBS	Garlic fresh-chopped
3	TBS	Dry red wine cold

Put in casing.

For hot Italian add:
1	TBS	Hot chili flakes or more

Breakfast Sausages Pork

Grind with medium 3/16" disk:

2.5	kg	Pork shoulder (20% fat is good)
500	gms.	Bacon (cheap fatty kind)

Spice mix:

2	TBS	Brown sugar
2	TBS	Ice water
4	tsp	Sage dried
4	tsp	Kosher salt
2	tsp	Black pepper

Mix in Kitchen Aid:

I just make patties, casings are too tough on a small sausage and I am too cheap to buy extra small casings.
Freeze on parchment and put in a Ziploc bag like IQF without the Q ha ha (individual quick frozen)

Venison Sausage

By John St. John Neumann and Dana Neumann

Base spice mix: if you are doing a lot

45	gms	Black pepper
42	gms	Cayenne Pepper
13	gms	Red chilies dried
11	gms	Basil
<u>106</u>	gms	Salt

217 gms in total

Grind or chop:

1500	gms	Onion
125	gms	Garlic
500	gms	Jalapeño

Use medium disk with grinder.

Base recipe:

In the Kitchen Aid Mix

1150	gms	Ground venison
450	gms	Ground bacon
35	gms	Spice mix
20	gms	Garlic
70	gms	Jalapeño pureed
235	gms	Onion
150	ml	Ice water

Maple version
Change quantities:

15	gms	Spice mix
45	gms	Garlic
no		Jalapeño
180	gms	Onion
150	gms	Maple syrup
1	tsp.	Black pepper
1	tsp.	Salt

For a manly twist add:

1/4	cup	Jack Daniels instead of ice water

Desserts

Bacon Chocolate Cake

Created for my carnivore editor Cindy B

In the sifter add (weird I know but it gets sifted twice)

1 ½	cups	Flour presifted
1 ½	cups	Sugar
6	TBS	Coco Powder
2	tsp.	Baking powder
1	tsp.	Salt

Mix this dry stuff until even

Add

2/3	cup	Soft lard
1	cup	Sour milk or buttermilk
2		Medium eggs

Pour in 2 x 8" cake pans
Bake until toothpick comes out clean
Let cool

Icing for middle of layers
Mix:

125	gms.	Cream cheese or Marscopapone Italian (soft)
45	gms.	Butter
1	cup	Icing Sugar
1	tsp.	Vanilla extract

Bacon Icing
Cook 6 slices of bacon and set aside reserve drippings

Chop;

225	gms.	bittersweet choc. chopped fine, put in bowl
1	TBS	Bacon drippings

Heat:

1	cup	35% cream to a boil, then immediately pour over choc.

Stir until all chocolate is melted
 Add: Bacon chopped Ps- don't eat the bacon it's for the icing.
Cool to room temp. Before icing your cake add candles, for the best man birthday cake.

Banana Bread

Cream:
120	gms	Butter or margarine
1	cup	Sugar

Add:
1		Egg
2		Mashed ripe bananas
2	TBS	Lemon juice
4	TBS	Milk

Sift together:
1 ½	cups	Flour
½	tsp.	Salt

Add:
¾	cup	Chopped nuts (your choice)

Add to wet ingredients and mix well
Place in loaf pan and bake at 350 for about an hour test with toothpick.

Optional: add bunches of chocolate chips, or chunks, or rosettes, or any shape of chocolate is good or raisins if you are health conscious.

Butter Tarts

In the Kitchen Aid:

1/2	cup	Brown sugar
1/4	cup	Corn syrup
45	gms	Butter soft
1		Egg
1/2	tsp	Vanilla
1/2	tsp	Vinegar

Make my pastry recipe: pg. 117
Cut circles to fit muffin pan 4-5"

Optional:

1/4	cup	Raisins or nuts or anything you like, added to the mixture.

Bake at 425 for 5 min
Then reduce temperature to 325 for another 10 min.

For my fellow chocoholics I secretly cover some with a chocolate ganache, don't tell anyone.

Caramel Crunch Brownies

Melt :
100	gms	Dark chocolate
115	gms.	Butter

Let cool slightly

Mix into chocolate:
1	cup	Sugar
2		Eggs
1	tsp	Vanilla
100	gms.	Flour
¼	tsp	Baking soda
	pinch	Salt

Bake for about 20 min in 8x8x2 pan with parchment, let it cool

Caramel layer:
Boil
115	gms	Butter
190	gms	Brown sugar
1	cup	Cream whipping 35%
1/2	cup	Corn syrup
1/2	tsp	Vanilla

Firm-ball (244 degrees F)

Chocolate topping
Chop fine:
| 200 | gms | Dark chocolate |

Heat until boiled
| 1/3 | cup | Cream whipping 35% |

Whisk the chocolate into cream until smooth.

Keep in refrigerator but serve warm to soften the caramel.

Pastry for Pies

Best one ever, thanks for this one Norma.

Mix:
1 ¾	cups (220 gms)	Flour
½	tsp.	Salt

Cut in:
1/3	lb.	Lard (cube in ½" pieces makes it faster)

The heat of your hands will make the dough tuff

Add: using a fork   Seven-Up until most of the dough comes off the sides of the bowl

Now use your hands to make a ball (do not knead)
It will roll out just fine.

Now it's up to you to choose your favorite pie filling.

For a brown top crust brush with an egg wash or milk

Chocolate Pecan Pie

This just happens to be my favorite.

Make Pastry recipe (previous page) roll and place in pie baking dish

Cover bottom with Pecan halves

In the Kitchen Aid:

Mix:
150	gms	Butter soft
200	gms	Brown Sugar
3		Eggs
½	cup	Honey
½	cup	Corn Syrup

Pour over pecans and bake until the jiggle in the center is about 2" wide about an hour.

Chocolate truffle

Melt:
300	gms	Chocolate (best dark you can get) in a double boiler

Add:
100	gms	Butter while the chocolate is melting –

Carefully stir in:
50	ml.	Whipping cream (not whipped) (115 gms)
2		Egg yolks

Pour over pie when cooled
Now make a dentist appointment ha ha

Chocolate Mousse Cake

By my Chef buddy Al (no last name).

CHOCOLATE CAKE
Preheat oven to 325 - grease and flour 2 x 9" cake pans
Sift together in a bowl & mix:

2	cups	Flour
¾	cup	Cocoa
2	cups	Sugar
1	tsp.	Baking powder
2	tsp.	Baking soda
1	tsp.	Salt

Then add & mix on medium speed for 2 min

1	cup	Veg oil,
1	cup	Milk
1	cup	Hot coffee

Then add & mix for 2 min

2		Eggs
1	tsp.	Vanilla

Pour evenly into pans 2 8" cake pans & bake about 30 min until done (toothpick clean)

THE CHOCOLATE MOUSSE
Melt:

225	grms	Dark chocolate (good stuff)
115	gms	Butter soft & mix in completely,

As it's cooling then slowly add in:

4		Egg yokes whisked (reserve whites)

Make meringue (cold bowl) - mix to soft peaks

1/2	cup	Egg whites, then add
38	gms.	Sugar & mix to stiff but moist peaks then fold into chocolate mix

Whip:

½	cup	35% cream to med peaks, then fold into the mix put in between cold cake layers

CHOCOLATE GANACHE
Chop:

225	gms.	Chocolate dark chopped fine, put in bowl

Heat:

1	cup	35% cream to a boil, then immediately pour over chocolate to cover

after 30 secs. whisk until smooth & creamy,
add:

1	TBS	Booze if you wish to add flavour

After cooling to a spreadable thickness, evenly ice the cake.

Pecan Pie Muffins

Mix:
- 1 cup Brown sugar
- ½ cups Flour

Add:
- 2 cups Pecans chopped

Beat in the mixer
- 2/3 cup Butter softened
- 2 Eggs

Add dry to wet until just mixed

Put in muffin pan with paper cup liners

Bake for 17 min
Cool muffins in the pan (they don't look cooked, but they are supposed to be gooey)

Carrot Pineapple Muffins

Thanks Dad.

Shred and drain:

1	cup	Carrots
1	cup	Pineapple

Mix:

1	cup	Sugar
2/3	cup	Vegetable oil
2	large	Eggs
1	tsp.	Vanilla

Separately mix:

1 ½	cup	Flour
2	tsp.	Baking powder
1	tsp.	Baking soda
1	tsp.	Cinnamon
1	tsp.	Nutmeg
½	tsp.	Salt

Bake until toothpick is clean

Chocolate Truffle

In my opinion you can put this on just about anything.

Melt:
450	gms	Chocolate (best dark you can get) in a double boiler

Add:
150	gms	Butter while the chocolate is melting –

Carefully stir in:

50	ml.	Whipping cream (not whipped) (115 gms)
2		Egg yolks

Or make truffle balls, or freeze for another time.

Chocolate Truffle Cheesecake

Bring to room temperature:
900   gms   Cream cheese

THE CRUST
Mix:
1 ¾   cups   Graham wafer crumbs
1/3   cup   Sugar
100   gms   Butter melted
Press into bottom of 10" spring form and bake for 4 min at 450

In the Kitchen Aid:
Mix:
1   cup   Sugar
½   cup   Cocoa

Add until smooth:
900   gms   Cream cheese

Add:
4   Eggs one at a time
1 ¼   cups   Sour Cream
1   tsp.   Vanilla

Melt and add:
160   gms   Chocolate Truffle
Mix gently until smooth

Pour over crust and bake at for 40 min or the jiggle in the middle is about 3"

Notes:
Cooking with a water bath will help with the cracking, also stage the cooling by turning off the oven open the door, then move to cooling rack on counter then in the fridge. Buuuuuut, if you are pouring Truffle over it who cares.

Melt:
170   gms   Chocolate truffle   (previous page)

Pour over cake and chill
Use a hot wet knife to slice.

Cinnamon Buns

Oven at 325
The Dough:
Warm to about 100 degrees

1	cup	Whole milk

Add: and let sit for 5 min

2 ½	tsp.	Dry yeast
¼	tsp.	Sugar

Whisk in:

60	gms	Butter melted
1		Egg yoke (large)
1 ½	tsp.	Vanilla

Whisk:

3	cups?	Flour
¾	tsp.	Salt
¼	cup	Sugar
½	tsp.	Nutmeg (grated)

In the kitchen Aid use dough hook and add the liquid slowly
Knead for 6 min (the dough should be on the sticky side but firm enough to be on the hook, adjust) Remove, oil the bowl and let stand to double in size.

Roll out the dough on a slightly floured surface in a rectangle with the longer side facing you 10x16

Filling:
Spread

¾	cup	Butter (soft) leaving ½" of space at top that you brush with water to seal.

Mix and sprinkle

½	cup	Brown sugar
3	TBS	Cinnamon

Its ok to up the sugar and cinnamon.

Roll up the dough away from you and press along edge to seal.
Cut into 2" rounds (about 8 buns)

Butter a 9x13 pan (I used glass) sprinkle Brown sugar to lightly coat bottom
Place: Pecans (coarsely chopped) on bottom
Then the rounds of dough cut side down

Cover with plastic wrap and let rise until doubled (should fill the pan) if they are not big and puffy wait longer

Bake in 325 degrees for 35 minutes
Cool the pan 15 min then cut around edges and remove the buns upside down.

Fruit Cobbler Crisp

This one is for you Cindy Bristow.

Peel and cube
4	cups	Fruit, anything you like or any combination even mangos

Mix:
1	cup	Flour
¾	cup	Rolled oats
1	cup	Brown sugar
1	tsp.	Cinnamon
115	gms	Butter, melted

In a medium sauce pan:
Cook until clear and thick about 10 min
½	cup	Sugar
1	TBS	Cornstarch
½	cup	Water
½	tsp.	Vanilla extract

Press half the oat mixture into a 9x13" baking dish. Cover with sliced fruit.
Pour sauce over. Cover with remaining crumble mixture.
Bake in oven 45 minutes, or until bubbly and golden.

Lemon Meringue Pie

By Penny's Mom.

Separate:
3		Eggs and let the whites come to room temperature

Preheat oven to 375 degrees

CRUST:
Melt:
75	gms	Butter

Mix:
1 ¼	cups	Graham wafer crumbs
¼	cup	Sugar
Add:	the	Melted butter

Spread in a 9" pie pan and bake at 375 degrees for 5 min.
Reduce the oven temp to 350 for the pie

FILLING
Beat:
3		Egg yokes until lemon yellow and thick

ADD UNTIL JUST MIXED (do not over beat)

2	cups	Eagle brand sweetened condensed milk about 2- 300 ml cans
1/3	cup	Lemon juice about 2 lemons

Pour into the cooled piecrust and start the meringue

MERINGUE

BEAT on High
3		Egg whites
½	tsp	Vanilla
¼	tsp	Cream of tarter

When soft peaks form

Add:
4	TBS	Sugar

and continue beating until stiff peaks form
Top the pie and seal the edges with the meringue

Bake for 15 min. Then cool and refrigerate for 4 hours

No Bake Cheesecake

The day before is a good idea.

First thing is make sure you have on a red t-shirt for the raspberry glaze part.

Graham Wafer crust -- Or Oreo crust: 8" or 9" spring form

Mix and put on bottom of pan

1 ½	cup	Crumbs
2	TBS	Sugar
75	gms	Butter (melted)

Bake at 375 for 5 min

Filling:
In the kitchen aid with beater paddle whip until smooth and fluffy

| 250 | gms | Cream cheese (room temp.) |

add slowly

1	can (300ml)	Eagle brand sweetened condensed milk
1/3	cup	Lemon juice
1	tsp.	Vanilla extract

When bottom is cool put filling in and chill for minimum 3 hrs.

Topping:
Melt in saucepan

2	cups	Frozen or fresh berries seeds removed (oh come on use a course sieve)
		I like raspberries with Sambuca for this one.
¼	cup	Water

Add

| 1 | TBS | Sugar |
| 1 | TBS | Corn starch |

Cook until thickened and clear.
Cool for 3 hrs.

Now stir in 3 TBS of your favorite liqueur.
Pour on top of cake and set in fridge.

Best to slice with a hot wet knife when serving.

Queen Elizabeth Cake

Pour:
1	cup	boiling water over
1	cup	Dates

Cream
60	gms	Butter
1	cup	White sugar

then add
2		eggs and mix

Add:

1 ¾	cups	Four
¼	tsp.	Salt
1	tsp.	Baking soda
1	tsp.	Baking powder

Add:
The softened Dates
½	cup	Walnuts

Mix well and pour into 9X13 pan
Bake at 350 for 25 min

Icing:
Bring to boil and cook for 3 min
2	cup	Brown sugar
2/3	cup	Butter
1/2	cup	Milk
1	cup	Coconut shredded (sweet) Optional

Spread over top and serve when cool

Drinks

Sangria

It's the best ever, that's why its in here. Thanks Hacienda Dos Gringos Restaurant.

In a 3-liter container or bigger, a small cooler with a tap works best

Add:
375	ml.	Seven – Up
375	ml.	Soda Water
1		Banana sliced
1		Lime chopped and squeeze juice in
1		Lemon chopped and squeeze juice in
1		Orange chopped and squeeze juice in
375	ml.	Pineapple canned with juice (crushed sliced whatever)
1500	ml.	Red wine cheap and harsh (a good wine does not make good Sangria)
3-5	oz.	Orange Liquor your favourite. (Triple sec, Grand Marnier etc.)

Mix all together and soak for minimum 24 hours.
Strain the solids out (don't go all OCD just a sieve will get the big bits out)
Now just drink it!!! The Sangria of course
Throw away the soaked fruit ... It's not pleasant
Garnish with fresh fruit.

Note: you can make white Sangria by using duh you ready for this one, "WHITE WINE"

Ice Cap

Tim Hortonish

In the blender:
100	gms	Espresso coffee cooled
70	gms	Cream (your choice)
1	TBS	Sugar heaping or add to your taste
140	gms	Ice

Beat on high until smooth.

A shot of Baileys Irish Cream, or Kahlua will wow this coffee.

Index

B

Bacon Chocolate Cake, 113
Banana Bread, 114
Beef Chili, 69
Beef Korma, 73
Beef Thai Basil, 72
Black Bean Salsa, 51
Blackened Shrimp, 14
Blackened Spice mix, 5
Bratwurst Sausage, 108
Breakfast Sausages Pork, 110
Brie Asparagus & Champagne, 46
Brownies, 116
Butter Chicken, 74
Butter Tarts, 115

C

Cajun BBQ Corn, 62
Cajun Curry Spice Mix, 7
Cajun Sausage, 107
Caribbean Pork Tenderloin, 75
Caribbean Spice Rub, 5
Carrot Pineapple Muffins, 121
Carrots Flambéed in Tequila, 66
Cheese and Spinach Pie, 12
Chicken Big Mamou, 77
Chicken Big Mamou Pasta, 86
Chicken Curry, 79
Chicken Noodle Soup, 43
Chicken on a Stick, 76
Chicken Shake Spice, 5
Chili Rellenos, 71
Chocolate Mousse Cake, 119
Chocolate Pecan Pie, 118
Chocolate Truffle, 122
Chocolate Truffle Cheesecake, 123
Cinnamon Buns, 124
Coconut Shrimps, 16
Corn Tortillas, 36
Cornbread, 15
Country Style Bread, 33
Cream Soups, 45
Creole Sauce, 52
Curry, 53

D

Dirty Rice, 80

E

Enchilada Sauce, 54

F

Fiesta Chicken, 81
Fish Chowder, 47
Fish Fillets Thai, 84
Fish Fry Batter, 83
Flour Tortillas, 37
Fried Chicken Quepos, 82
Fried Yardbird, 89
Fruit Cobbler Crisp, 125

G

Garam Masala, 6
Garam Tandoori, 6
Garlic King Sauce, 55
Greek Garlic Chicken, 90
Greek Salad Dressing, 24
Gringo Spice Mix, 4
Gumbo with Cajun Sausage, 48

H

Ham Steaks with Jack Daniels, 91
House Salad Dressing, 25
Huevos Mexicana, 9

I

Ice Cap, 131
Italian Sausage, 109

J

Jamaican Jerk Spice Rub, 6

L

Lamb Shanks, 92
Lasagna a la Cindy, 93
Lemon Chicken, 94
Lemon Meringue Pie, 126

M

Mac and Cheese, 95

Follow that Food

Mamou Spice Mix, 7
Mango Chicken Salad, 29
Manicotti, 96
Meatballs, 88
Mild Salsa, 56
Mild Salsa Spice Mix, 4
Montreal vinaigrette Dressing, 23
Muffuletta Olive Salad, 28

N

No Bake Cheesecake, 127

O

Onion Bhaji, 17

P

Pastry for Pies, 117
Pecan Pie Muffins, 120
Peking Duck, 97
Peppered Pork, 85
Picco de Gallo Salsa, 56
Pizza Dough, 38
Pork Satay, 18
Pork Tenderloin, 98
Portuguese Bread, 34
Potato and Egg Omelet, 10
Potatoes, 64

Q

Queen Elizabeth Cake, 128

R

Ranch Salad Dressing, 26
Red Lobster Biscuits, 40

Roasted Spuds, 65

S

Salmon Dave's Pasta, 99
Samosas, 19
Sangria, 130
Scalloped Potatoes, 63
Scones Coffeehouse, 39
Smoked Salmon, 21
Soups, 42
Spaghetti with Italian Sausage, 100
Spanakopita, 101
Spinach Frittata, 11
Spinach Quesadillas, 102
Spring Rolls, 20
Stir Fry Sauce, 57

T

Tabbouleh, 67
Tacos el Pastor, 103
Thai Chicken, 87
Thai Yum Salad Dressing, 27
Tomato Sauce, 59
Tortilla Soup, 44

V

Vegetable Chili, 70
Venison Meatloaf, 104
Venison Sausage, 111
V-H Sauce, 60

W

White Sauce, 50
Whole Wheat Bread, 35
Wing Ding Salad, 30

ABOUT THE AUTHOR

Once upon a long time ago, I was a kid just going into high school with the world before me.

My dad owned a beauty salon and rented the basement to a printing company. Well let me tell you, when I first laid eyes on all that equipment, the gadgets, the paper and ink, I just knew this was the life for me. So I hung around and begged them to let me help at no wage at all. Sure enough my perseverance paid off and didn't they let me into the shop! I worked every night after school and on the weekends. After my first year the owners finally decided that they could no longer take advantage of my free labor and made the decision to pay me for my summer job. I remember looking back and thinking, getting paid for something you loved and couldn't get enough of. Of course it seemed like a lot of money until I divided it by the hours I worked there……. I think it worked out to be about 24 cents an hour but I was certainly not complaining. I learned a ton of information from those guys. (All of this made me the worst smart aleck in my printing class at school!) For the next 22 years I moved up to the top of my profession.

In my 20's I took off for Europe for a couple of months between jobs to see the world. Whilst in Germany I met the most interesting man. He was walking down the street towards me wearing a cream colored suit with a leather briefcase and he stopped and asked me if I wear a watch. 'Sure of course I do, why, you need the time?' We spent about half an hour talking, and the words he spoke changed me forever. He told me to lose the watch, it is controlling you, and he also told me I should change careers at least 3 times in my life to be happy. I never forgot that guy and took his advice.

When I was about 34, at the top of my game, I realized I was getting bored with printing. The challenge and learning were over. This was a critical point in my life where I understood that when the brain sponge is full you just can't stuff more data in there. The only cure for this is to change careers and get a new sponge. So I talked it over with my girlfriend and explained my dream was to open a restaurant "What do you think Cindy?" At this time she had been working in the industry for years and told me outright it was a bad idea and don't do it. But in the end she came around and helped me with setting it up and running the place. So I did my research and crunched the numbers found a decrepit restaurant for sale and took the plunge.

I had no experience in this business but I had an idea that was sound. How about I cook the best food from the freshest ingredients with no short cuts? People will give us money and come back for more. Well fellow foodies it worked for 20 years. When times got tough I didn't look for ways to cut cost I upped the grade of my raw ingredients and made the portions bigger. Wow go figure that worked too. You see its like this, if you have a disappointing meal at a restaurant you never go back and you tell all your friends not to go for that overpriced crap food… however if you loved your meal it works the other way, you tell all your friends and you can't really remember how much it cost you because everybody knows good food costs money and you are definitely going back.

Next; after my run in the restaurant business, I kind of slid sideways by chance into the construction industry. I have always been around it with my Dad renovating apartments, my uncle George was a cabinetmaker and doing my house over, of course I did all the renovations to the restaurant a few times. So it was an easy transition (not like the restaurant). One of the regulars in the bar (Scott) asked me to help out on a renovation job. Well to date I haven't looked back.

That's not really true at all, I look back all the time at my life and think what a lucky guy I have been to love what I did through all of it. Semi retired now living at the lake in our small 4-season cottage and wintering in Mexico life can't possibly get any better.

So thank you all my friends for buying my cookbook and I hope you get as much enjoyment from it as I did cooking all of them and writing it…Cheers